KEITH
FLOYD

COGNAC COOKERY

PENGUIN BOOKS

PENGUIN BOOKS

Published by the Penguin Group, Penguin Books Ltd, 27 Wrights Lane, London
w8 5tz, England. Penguin Books USA Inc., 375 Hudson Street, New York, New
York 10014, USA. Penguin Books Australia Ltd, Ringwood, Victoria, Australia.
Penguin Books Canada Ltd, 10 Alcorn Avenue, Toronto, Ontario, Canada m4v
3b2. Penguin Books (NZ) Ltd, 182–190 Wairau Road, Auckland 10, New Zealand
· Penguin Books Ltd, Registered Offices: Harmondsworth, Middlesex, England ·
These recipes have been selected from *Floyd on France*, published by BBC Books
and from *Far Flung Floyd*, *Floyd on Africa*, *Floyd on Hangovers*, and *Floyd on Spain*,
first published by Michael Joseph in 1993, 1996, 1992 and 1992 respectively. *Floyd
on Hangovers* published by Signet in 1993. *Far Flung Floyd*, *Floyd on Oz* and *Floyd
on Spain* published by Penguin Books in 1994, 1992 and 1993 respectively. This
edition published 1996. Copyright © Keith Floyd, 1992, 1993, 1994, 1996. All rights
reserved · The moral right of the author has been asserted.

CONTENTS

Foreword

In the seventeenth century, the wines from the Cognac area were so much in demand that their quality deteriorated and they did not travel as well as before. The Dutch traders and Scandinavians too decided to boil the thin white wine of the Cognac region to reduce its volume and called it 'burnt wine'. It was cognac in its crudest form. However, it was the British who were responsible for recognizing the potential of the world's finest 'digestif'.

It was first noted as cognac brandy in *The London Gazette* of 1678.

The grapes are picked when barely ripe to make a fairly thin, harsh wine, high in acidity and low in alcohol and it is distilled twice. It takes about ten bottles of wine to make one of cognac. It is then aged in weathered oak casks.

Some of the finest of cognac will have been matured for at least twenty years in the cask, some possibly more than forty years. Once bottled, the drink is stable and will not change with time.

I have a great fondness for 'brandy', be it a humble marc or a grande fine champagne cognac (which incidentally has nothing to do with champagne in this context, the word champagne refers to flat, chalky countryside) and I recall many years ago an occasion during a period of temporary penury when my dog ate the haunch of wild boar I had marinated in, among other things, red wine and half a bottle of cognac. I was obliged to dine from a plate of simple pasta flavoured only with olive oil. However, my chagrin and dismay evaporated into mellowness when, with my last remaining 20 franc note, I ordered 'une grande fine' at the Café de France along with 'un express'. After savouring the heavenly aroma and sipping slowly this fine, smooth nectar I quite convinced myself that I had dined superbly.

Cognac – I salute you!

Hors d'Oeuvres and Light Dishes

LIGHTLY CURRIED PUMPKIN AND APPLE SOUP

from FLOYD ON AFRICA

This excellent soup was served to me at the Imba Matombo
Lodge, near Harare.

SERVES 4

25 ml (1 fl oz) sunflower oil
15 g (½ oz) butter
1 large onion, chopped
450 g (1 lb) butternut squash, peeled and cubed
200 g (7 oz) peeled and cubed potato
2 medium eating apples, peeled and cubed
½ teaspoon ground turmeric
1 teaspoon curry powder
½ teaspoon ground cinnamon
½ teaspoon ground ginger
750 ml (1¼ pints) chicken stock
½ teaspoon salt
1 bay leaf
small pinch of sugar

100 ml (4 fl oz) milk
25 ml (1 fl oz) cognac

To serve:

whipped or soured cream
a little paprika or 1 tablespoon chopped fresh
*   chives*

Heat the oil and butter in a large pan, add the onion and sauté until golden. Add the squash, potato, apples and spices and toss together over a low heat for about 2 minutes, until the fruit and vegetables are coated and the aromas of the spices are released. Add the stock, salt, bay leaf and sugar, bring to the boil, cover and simmer gently for about 25 minutes until the vegetables are soft.

Cool until lukewarm, then remove the bay leaf. Purée the soup in a blender until absolutely smooth. Reheat gently in a clean pan, adding just enough milk to give a medium-thick consistency. Add the cognac and heat through without boiling. Ladle the soup into warmed bowls, top each one with a little cream and dust with paprika or sprinkle with chopped chives. (From Zimbabwe.)

BASS SOUFFLÉ WITH PRAWN SAUCE
Soufflé de Bar au Coulis de Langoustine

from FLOYD ON FRANCE

This is a superb dish from my friend Claude Arnaud of Le Saint-Hubert at Saint-Saturnin d'Apt.

SERVES 4

For the soufflé:

300 g (10 oz) fillet of bass, chopped
salt and pepper
1 egg white
250 ml (8 fl oz) double cream
pinch of cayenne pepper

For the prawn sauce:

75 ml (3 fl oz) oil
1 kg (2 lb) langoustines
2 carrots, chopped
½ onion, finely chopped
1 shallot, finely chopped
1 clove garlic, crushed

75 ml (3 fl oz) cognac
300 ml (10 fl oz) white wine
1 teaspoon tomato purée
3 tomatoes, crushed
1 bouquet garni
salt and pepper
450 ml (15 fl oz) double cream
tarragon

First prepare the sauce. Heat the oil in a flameproof casserole dish. Add the langoustines and leave for 5 or 6 minutes. Remove from the pan, shell them and set aside.

Put the carrots, onion, shallot and garlic into the casserole and add the langoustine shells. Pour in the cognac and flame. Leave covered for 3 or 4 minutes.

Add the wine to the casserole, along with the tomato purée, the crushed tomatoes, bouquet garni, salt and pepper. Leave to boil for 10 minutes. Next add the double cream and tarragon and leave to simmer for another 10 minutes. Finally, strain the sauce through a fine sieve. (There is too much sauce for four, but it's not worth making less, so freeze half for another occasion.)

Pre-heat the oven to gas mark 4, 180°C (350°F).

To make the soufflé, put the chopped fish, salt and pepper into a food processor for about 3 minutes. Add the egg white and mix again for 1 minute. Refrigerate this mixture for about 30 minutes. Return to the food processor, adding the cream, little by little. Finally add a pinch of cayenne pepper.

Bake in the oven in a *bain-marie* for 20 minutes. Serve immediately. Pour the sauce on a large dinner plate, place the soufflé on the sauce and surround with the langoustines. (From Provence.)

TRUFFLE OMELETTE
Omelette aux Truffes

from FLOYD ON FRANCE

SERVES 2

1 fresh or preserved truffle
50 ml (2 fl oz) cognac
4 eggs
50 ml (2 fl oz) double cream
salt and pepper
1 tablespoon goose fat

If using a fresh truffle carefully brush clean and wash it. Slice finely and steep for 1 hour in the cognac. Add 50 ml

(2 fl oz) water and bring to the boil. Allow to cool before using. Reserve the cooking liquid.

If using a preserved truffle, simply marinate it for 1 hour in the cognac. Reserve the marinade.

Separate 1 of the eggs and beat the white until stiff. Beat the yolk with the rest of the eggs, together with the cream, salt, pepper and 1 tablespoon truffle cooking liquid or marinade. At the last minute, carefully fold in the egg white and truffle slices, reserving a few for decoration. Melt the goose fat in a shallow frying pan. When it begins to smoke, pour in the eggs. Cook over a high heat. When done, fold in half and slide on to a platter.

Mind you, my friends, Mme Moulin, a Périgord landlady of my acquaintance, would not agree with this recipe – she wouldn't put truffles into an omelette for a start. She'd rather have ceps and make the omelette really thick and heavy. In fact, when I cooked her a light fluffy cep one, she scolded me unmercifully!! (From Périgord.)

FRESH FOIE GRAS WITH TRUFFLES

Pâté de Foie Gras aux Truffes

from FLOYD ON FRANCE

Foie gras is the food of kings and Arab princes – and also the French, especially at Christmas time. Sadly, the method of preparing this great delicacy is rather barbaric (the force-feeding of the geese to produce the abnormally large liver). The farmers, of course, deny any cruelty. And I must admit that it has never stopped me from enjoying it. Sorry.

SERVES 8

*1 large pink foie gras (goose liver), skinned, blood
 vessels removed
½ glass good cognac
15 g (½ oz) salt for each 500 g (1 lb) foie gras
white pepper
200 g (7 oz) pork fat
1 truffle, well washed and finely sliced*

Put the goose liver in a bowl and add half the cognac, salt and pepper. Gently knead it to allow the cognac to 9 penetrate. Chill for 24 hours. Add the rest of the cognac and return to the refrigerator for 1 hour.

Pre-heat the oven to gas mark 6, 200°C (400°F).

Meanwhile, line a terrine with the pork fat. Push the liver into the terrine. Slice the liver down the middle lengthways with a very sharp knife and push the truffle slivers about half-way down into it. Close the liver opening and cover with pork fat. Cover the terrine and cook in a *bain-marie* in the oven for 35 minutes. The water temperature should not exceed 80°C (176°F). Refrigerate and serve completely cool. (From Périgord.)

COUNTRY TERRINE
Pâté de Campagne

from FLOYD ON FRANCE

The simple French country terrine, if made at home with fresh ingredients and served chilled with a few gherkins, some olives and some sweet summer tomatoes, is one of the finest hors d'oeuvres there is. Recipes vary from area to area, but they are all roughly based on pork, veal and pig's liver, and they tend to be quite fatty and crumbly, which is nice. Here is a typical version.

SERVES 4 – 8

500 g (1 lb) belly of pork, finely chopped not
   minced
250 g (8 oz) pig's liver, minced
350 g (12 oz) veal, minced
125 g (4 oz) sheet of pork fat
   or slice of speck (cured pork fat), half cut into
   1-cm (½-in.)-thick strips and half cut into little
   cubes
2 cloves garlic, crushed
6 black peppercorns, crushed
4 juniper berries, crushed
pinch of ground mace
salt and pepper
1 large glass dry white wine
1 generous splash cognac

Pre-heat the oven to gas mark 3, 160°C (325°F).

Mix everything except the strips of fat together and leave
to stand for a couple of hours in a cool place.

Tip the lot into a terrine and lay the strips of fat over
the top. Put the terrine in a *bain-marie* and cook in the
oven for about 1½ hours. Leave to cool for 24 hours before
eating.

Fish and Shellfish

SCALLOP TIMBALES
Timbales de Coquilles St Jacques

from FLOYD ON FRANCE

SERVES 6

500 g (1 lb) white fish fillets, skinned
185 ml (6½ fl oz) double cream
1 teaspoon salt
½ coffeespoon pepper
3 egg whites, beaten until stiff
50 g (2 oz) butter
275 g (9 oz) scallops
pinch of cayenne pepper
1 clove garlic, finely chopped
1 tablespoon parsley, finely chopped
1 tablespoon tomato purée
Shellfish Sauce (see page 13)
Cooked pastry shapes to decorate

Pre-heat the oven to gas mark 2, 150°C (300°F).

First purée the fish fillets in a liquidizer and put them into a cold mixing bowl. Stir in 125 ml (4 fl oz) of the cream, season with salt and pepper and fold in the egg whites. Butter the insides of six timbales (ramekins) and partly fill with the fish mixture. Make a hole in the mixture through which later to insert the scallops. Save enough of the mixture to cover the timbales when the scallops have been added.

Fry the scallops gently in butter with the cayenne, garlic and parsley and add the tomato purée and the remaining cream. Divide among the timbales and cover with the reserved fish mixture. Poach in a *bain-marie* for 30 minutes.

Tip out of the timbales and serve hot with Shellfish Sauce. Decorate the dish with little pastry shapes.

SHELLFISH SAUCE

This is a great sauce for things like fish terrines and plain white fish fillets.

SERVES 6

25 g (1 oz) onion, finely chopped
25 g (1 oz) carrot, finely chopped

25 g (1 oz) butter
6 freshwater crayfish with shells on or the
  crushed-up shell of 1 lobster
250 ml (8 fl oz) cognac
50 ml (2 fl oz) dry white wine
600 ml (1 pint) fish velouté
50 g (2 oz) tomatoes, chopped
15 g (½ oz) tomato purée
salt and pepper

Fry the onion and carrot in butter until they turn golden. Add the crayfish, or pieces of lobster shell. Flame with the cognac and pour in the white wine. Let this mixture reduce by about a third. Add the fish velouté and simmer gently. Next add the tomatoes and tomato purée, salt and pepper, and cook for a further 30 minutes.

Whack the whole lot through a food processor or liquidizer and strain through a very fine sieve.

CRAYFISH BISQUE

from FLOYD ON AFRICA

Please remember that all cooking times and measurements should be taken with a large pinch of salt! The food is cooked only when you are happy with it and not because the recipe says so.

SERVES 8

250 ml (9 fl oz) vegetable oil
3 kg (6½ lb) chopped live crayfish (include the shells and heads)
butter
4 carrots, diced
2 sticks of celery, chopped
3 onions, diced
2 leeks, chopped
1 garlic bulb, chopped
250 ml (9 fl oz) cognac
1 bottle of white wine
275 g (10 oz) tomato purée
15 very ripe plum tomatoes, halved
2 bay leaves

4 sprigs of fresh thyme
4 litres (7 pints) fish or chicken stock
a little mashed potato to thicken (if necessary)
salt and freshly ground black pepper

Heat the oil in a large pan until it is smoking. Add the chopped crayfish and cook hard until they take colour. Turn down the heat, add a little butter and put in the carrots, celery, onions, leeks and garlic. Sweat for 2 minutes or so.

Pour on the cognac and flame. Add the wine and reduce by half. Add the tomato purée and cook until the sauce thickens. Add the fresh tomatoes, herbs and stock. Cover and cook gently for ¾ – 1 hour. If necessary thicken with a little mashed potato. Put through a fine sieve, check the seasoning and serve. (From South Africa.)

SHRIMPS FLAMBÉED IN COGNAC

Crevettes Flambées

from FLOYD ON FRANCE

SERVES 6

3 tablespoons butter
500 g (1 lb) live grey shrimps
1 glass cognac

Melt the butter and, when it is bubbling, throw in the shrimps and toss them for 3 minutes over a medium heat. Add the cognac and flame. Serve immediately. (From Charente.)

LOBSTER WITH CHICKEN
Langosta con Pollo

from FLOYD ON SPAIN

SERVES 4

4 tablespoons olive oil

1.25 kg (3 lb) free-range, corn-fed chicken,
jointed into small pieces (buy one with giblets
and reserve the liver)

1 live lobster weighing about 1 kg (2¼ lb) – get
your fishmonger to kill it for you if you're
squeamish. Ask him to divide it into pieces, and
remind him you need the green liver bit

1 medium onion, chopped

3 tablespoons cognac

250 ml (8 fl oz) dry white wine

4 medium tomatoes, skinned and chopped

1 bay leaf

½ teaspoon fresh thyme

pared zest of ½ orange

2 tablespoons chopped fresh parsley

2 cloves of garlic, crushed

75 g (3 oz) blanched almonds

75 g (3 oz) hazelnuts

1½ teaspoons grated dark chocolate

a few strands of saffron

300 ml (½ pint) fish stock – this can be made by
   boiling the lobster's small claws and head in
   salted water for ½ an hour

salt

freshly ground black pepper

Heat the oil in a large frying pan. Pop in the chicken pieces and fry them quite briskly for 4 to 5 minutes, until nicely browned. Transfer them to a large casserole dish.

Now the lobster. Cook the tail and large claws in the same frying pan for a couple of minutes until pink, then lift out and put the pieces with the chicken.

Add the chopped onion to the pan and sauté until golden and well reduced, then stir in the cognac, wine, tomatoes, bay leaf, thyme, orange zest and 1 tablespoon of the parsley. Stir well and simmer gently for at least 15 minutes to reduce.

Stir this mixture into the casserole with the chicken and lobster and pop it into a preheated oven, gas mark 5, 190°C (375°F), for 10 minutes while you do the next bit.

You can either pound together the garlic, nuts, chocolate and saffron with the chicken and lobster livers in the time-honoured way or you can whizz everthing together in a blender, adding a little fish stock to make a paste. However you do it, you must stir the results with the lobster and chicken in the casserole dish, adding the rest of the fish stock. Season with some salt and pepper and leave to cook, covered, for another 15–20 minutes.

Fish out the orange zest, if it is still in one piece, and bay leaf. Garnish with the remaining chopped parsley and serve.

HAKE IN COGNAC

Merluza en Coñac

from FLOYD ON SPAIN

Hake, which is in the same family as haddock and cod, is probably Spain's most popular fish. And there are lots of them off the Mediterranean coast and in the Bay of Biscay. Or rather there used to be. But now, because of the global warming thing everyone is wittering on about, hake are migrating further north and, much to the consternation of British and Irish fishermen, the old hake have upsticked and taken residence in the Irish Sea, which has become warmer.

But to go back to the recipe. Fresh hake is marvellous and whether you just grill it and serve with some parsley sauce or even pan-fry a fillet with a little butter and lemon, you can't beat it. I invented this recipe in a moment of desperation on the harbour wall at Andraitx, to celebrate our happy sojourn in Majorca.

SERVES 4

4 × 175 g (6 oz) hake cutlets
3 or 4 saffron strands, crushed
4 tablespoons olive oil
1 onion, finely chopped
2 cloves of garlic, finely chopped
4 tomatoes, skinned and chopped
1 tablespoon chopped fresh parsley
3–4 tablespoons cognac
24 mussels, well scrubbed (throw out any damaged
    ones or ones that remain closed when tapped)
1 wineglass dry white wine
salt
freshly ground black pepper

Rinse the hake cutlets and pat them dry with kitchen paper, then rub the crushed saffron over them.

Heat the oil in a large frying pan and fry together the onion and garlic for about 10 minutes until softened. Tip in the tomatoes and parsley and cook for at least 30 minutes, so the tomatoes and onions liaise into a thick, rich sauce. Then pop in the fish steaks. Turn up the heat to really get them going, turning them over after 1 minute.

Cook for a minute or so on the second side, then add the cognac and mussels, closely followed by the wine. Season with some salt and pepper and simmer gently for 15 minutes.

Serve, strewn with some more parsley, with a bowl of buttered new potatoes and a crisp salad.

LEMON SOLE WITH WHITE WINE AND GRAPES

from FLOYD ON OZ

SERVES 4

100 g (4 oz) seedless white grapes, halved if large
1 tablespoon cognac
8 × 100–125 g (4–5 oz) lemon sole fillets,
    skinned

50 g (2 oz) butter
6 shallots or 1 large Spanish onion, finely chopped
300 ml (10 fl oz) fish stock or water
1 bay leaf
1 bouquet garni
4 tablespoons Australian dry white wine
1 tablespoon cornflour mixed with a little water
4 tablespoons double cream
salt
ground white pepper

Put the grapes into a bowl with the cognac, stir through and leave to soak for 20 minutes or so.

Rinse the sole fillets and pat dry with kitchen paper, then roll them up from the tail end and secure with cocktail sticks. Pop them into a buttered ovenproof dish.

Melt the butter in a small, heavy-based pan and fry the shallots or onion for about 3–4 minutes, until transparent. Reserve 2 tablespoons onion and set to one side, then add the fish stock or water, bay leaf and bouquet garni to the pan. Bring to the boil, then carefully pour over the rolled fish fillets. Cover and bake in a preheated oven, 180°C/350°F (gas mark 4), until tender.

When the fish is cooked, strain off the liquid and pour 150 ml (5 fl oz) into the small pan, adding the reserved onion. Discard any remaining liquid. Add the wine to the pan and heat gently until simmering. Thicken the liquid with the blended cornflour and cook for 1 minute more. Remove from the heat, then stir in the grapes and cream. Reheat very gently, but do not allow to boil. Taste and adjust the seasoning, then pour the sauce over the fish. Delicious served with creamed potatoes and lightly cooked broccoli.

PS Avoid the possibility of death by cocktail stick – remove before serving! (From Tasmania.)

FRIED FISH AND GINGER

from FAR FLUNG FLOYD

To my mind, bass is undoubtedly the king of fish, and a whole, crispy, deep-fried one is a gourmet's treat. But this dish would work equally well with inexpensive dabs or soles. The trick is to drizzle hot oil on to the ginger and spring onions so that they actually cook very lightly.

SERVES 4

2 tablespoons cognac
1 tablespoon light soy sauce

> *1 teaspoon brown sugar*
> *1 tablespoon sesame oil*
> *1 or 2 whole bass or grey mullet (weighing 900*
> *g [2 lb]), scaled, gutted and cleaned*
> *a little plain flour*
> *groundnut or sunflower oil for frying, about 150*
> *ml (¼ pint)*
> *1 tablespoon fresh root ginger, shredded*
> *2 tablespoons shredded spring onions*
> *1 red chilli pepper, seeded and finely sliced*

Mix together the cognac, soy sauce, sugar and sesame oil. With a sharp knife make several diagonal slashes on both sides of the bass. Lay the fish in a dish and pour over the marinade. Leave in a cool place for about an hour.

Drain the fish and dredge well with flour. Heat the oil until sizzling in a large wok or deep pan. Fry the fish for about 15–20 minutes, until crisp and tender. Carefully lift out the fish and place on a serving dish.

Sprinkle over the ginger and spring onions. Take some hot oil from the wok and drizzle 3 or 4 tablespoons of it over the ginger and spring onions. Garnish with the chilli. (From Thailand.)

Chicken and Game

PIGEON CASSEROLE
Salmis de Palombes

from FLOYD ON FRANCE

The Basquaises are a charming lot and their food is splendid.

One of their specialities is Pigeon Casserole, and very delicious it is too. But the way they catch the pigeons leaves a little to be desired in these enlightened times. Briefly, they net the little darlings! Très folklorique, no doubt, but actually quite barbarous. Still, this is a cookbook, not a Greenpeace pamphlet. So on with the recipe.

SERVES 4

2 plump young pigeons, cut in half
knob of butter
3 rashers fatty bacon, diced
2 onions, diced
1 glass cognac
2 tablespoons flour

26

1 large glass red wine
450 ml (15 fl oz) chicken stock
1 sprig of thyme
1 bay leaf
3 carrots, diced
Salt and pepper

Melt the butter in a pan and brown the pigeons on all sides. Remove from the pan. Add the bacon and onions and fry until golden. Return the pigeons to the pan, and flame in cognac. Now stir in the flour over the heat until it is well absorbed into the juices, pour in the wine and stock and boil for 5 minutes.

Add the herbs, carrots and seasoning, turn down the heat and simmer for about 1½ hours. Check that the pigeons are tender, transfer them to a hot serving dish and keep warm while you bubble up the sauce to reduce it until it is thick and rich. Strain off any excess fat and pour over the birds. (From Basque Country.)

RABBIT WITH PEARS AND TURNIPS

Conejo con Peras y Nabos

from FLOYD ON SPAIN

I have included this dish because of the fascinating combination of ingredients, namely rabbit and pears. A simple rabbit stew with carrots, onions and turnips – little baby ones, nicely peeled – cooked in stock would be a nice English way to prepare this. But the addition of pears and a drop of white wine lifts it out of the ordinary and into the exotic and amusing.

SERVES 4

1 rabbit, weighing about 1.25 kg (3 lb), jointed
2 tablespoons plain flour
salt
freshly ground black pepper
250 ml (8 fl oz) olive oil
½ wineglass cognac
1 wineglass dry white wine
250 ml (8 fl oz) chicken or rabbit stock or water
1 large onion, chopped

2 cloves of garlic, chopped

1 large carrot, roughly chopped

4 turnips, roughly chopped

1 leek, sliced

4 large pears, cored and quartered (do not peel)

1 ripe tomato, skinned and chopped

*a small bundle of fresh herbs – for example, thyme,
     rosemary, parsley and a bay leaf*

Roll the pieces of rabbit in the flour, which you have seasoned with some salt and pepper. Heat half the oil in a large flameproof casserole and fry the rabbit for about 10 minutes, until it is golden brown. Pour in the cognac and set fire to it with a match. When the flames have died down, pour in the wine and stock or water. Bubble away gently while you carry on in another pan.

Heat the rest of the oil and fry the onion, garlic, carrot, turnips, leek and two of the pears. When they are soft – about 8–10 minutes – pop in the tomato and bouquet garni. Tip this lot over the rabbit and carry on cooking, adding more liquid as it is needed, until the rabbit is really tender – about 1¼ hours should be fine. Ten minutes before serving, add the remaining two pears.

STUFFED PHEASANT

Faisan Farci à la Périgourdine

from FLOYD ON FRANCE

SERVES 4

500 g (1 lb) hen pheasant, giblets reserved
1 medium onion, chopped
75 g (3 oz) smoked bacon, diced
salt and pepper
75 g (3 oz) butter
50 ml (2 fl oz) nut oil
75 ml (3 fl oz) cognac
1 litre (2 pints) Verjus
1 bouquet garni (thyme, bay leaf and rosemary)
300 ml (10 fl oz) double cream
croutons

Stuff the pheasant with the onion, its giblets, half the bacon, salt and pepper and 1 tablespoon butter. Sew up the opening and brown the bird in oil and butter with the rest of the bacon in a flameproof casserole.

Flame with the cognac, add the Verjus and the bouquet garni. Cover and simmer for 30 minutes.

Uncover and reduce the sauce by a third, before stirring in the cream. Allow to thicken, season, and serve with the croutons and some potatoes sautéed in goose fat. (From Périgord.)

PARTRIDGE WITH MORELS

Perdrix aux Morilles

from FLOYD ON FRANCE

1 partridge per person, plucked, gutted, giblets
reserved
cognac
500 g (1 lb) fresh morels
150 g (5 oz) smoked bacon, diced
1 small onion per partridge
thyme
salt and pepper
2 tablespoons nut oil
150 g (5 oz) butter
1 lump sugar
300 ml (10 fl oz) double cream

Marinate the partridge giblets overnight in cognac. Stuff each bird with 1 morel, 2 pieces of bacon, half an onion, a pinch of thyme, salt and pepper and sew up the opening.

Brown the partridges in the oil and butter in a large flameproof casserole. Then add the rest of the bacon and the onions. When the onions have started to colour, flame with cognac. Throw in 300 ml (10 fl oz) water and the rest of the morels. Simmer for about 45 minutes until the sauce is well reduced, then stir in the sugar and cream and allow to thicken. Check the seasoning and serve. (From Périgord.)

GUINEA-FOWL WITH BACON IN WINE

from FLOYD ON AFRICA

SERVES 4

vegetable oil
450 g (1 lb) button onions
175 g (6 oz) thick bacon, cut into pieces
1 whole guinea-fowl, cut into eight (thighs,
  drumsticks, and halved breasts)

good splash of cognac
good splash of orange liqueur
½ bottle of red wine
50 g (2 oz) butter, cut into pieces
a few sprigs of fresh thyme
1 orange, cut into segments

Heat a little oil in a pan. Add the onions and cook until lightly browned and softened. Add the bacon pieces and brown. Remove from the pan and reserve. Add the guinea-fowl thighs and drumsticks and cook for a few minutes before adding the breasts. When the meat has browned, pour over the cognac and flame. Add the orange liqueur and red wine and simmer for about 20 minutes until the sauce has reduced and the guinea-fowl is tender. Remove the guinea-fowl from the pan and keep warm.

Whisk the butter into the sauce until it thickens slightly and becomes shiny. Return the onions and bacon to the pan, heat through, then spoon over the guinea-fowl. Sprinkle with thyme and garnish with orange segments. (From South Africa.)

DUCK PIE

Tourte de Canard à la Bourguignonne

from FLOYD ON FRANCE

SERVES 8

*1 × 2.25 kg (5 lb) duck, boned and jointed, liver
  reserved*
250 g (8 oz) fat pork, cut in bite-size chunks
250 g (8 oz) bacon, cut in bite-size chunks
*625 g (1¼ lb) lean pork, cut in bite-size
  chunks*
250 g (8 oz) chicken livers
1 egg yolk
Enough aspic to make up 1 litre (2 pints) liquid

For the marinade:

1 bottle white wine
3 teaspoons salt
1 teaspoon pepper
2 teaspoons allspice
300 ml (10 fl oz) port

34

50 ml (2 fl oz) cognac
6 shallots
Thyme and bay leaves

For the pastry:

750 g (1½ lb) flour, sifted
20 g (1 oz) salt
400 g (14 oz) lard, cut in pieces
3 eggs, beaten

Combine all the marinade ingredients. Divide between the meats and duck, adding the duck liver to the chicken livers, and marinate each separately for 48 hours in the refrigerator. Then drain, reserving the marinade.

Make the pastry. Mix the flour, salt and lard with your fingertips. Add the eggs and enough water to make a firm dough. Roll into a ball and refrigerate until ready to use.

Pre-heat the oven to gas mark 4, 180°C (350°F).

Divide the dough in two and line a deep baking dish with half of it. Put in one layer of drained meat and then one layer of drained duck. Repeat until the dish is nearly full. Close with a pastry lid, pinching the edges together well. Cut a small hole in the top. Decorate with the pastry trimmings and brush with egg yolk. Bake in the oven for 2½ hours. Leave to cool.

Then boil the strained marinade, add the aspic and allow to cool until it begins to thicken. Pour into the hole in the top of the pie. Refrigerate and serve when the aspic is firm.

OK, it's quite a lot of work. But it would make a splendid dish for, say, a Christmas Eve supper, along with a crisp winter salad, fine wines and about eight friends. (From Burgundy.)

COCKEREL IN RED WINE

Coq au Vin

from FLOYD ON FRANCE

Burgundy is supposed to be famous for Coq au Vin, but these days it's really hard to find an authentic one. In restaurants they vary from insipid chicken stewed in uncooked wine to mountainous piles of exaggerated culinary chauvinism. Here's how to do it properly, or rather it's a Floyd-adapted version of that of the redoubtable Mme LeClerc of the Hôtel du Terroit at Gevrey-Chambertin; where, by the way, she makes her 'kirs' with double crème de cassis and red Gevrey-Chambertin. They are amazing!!

2 kg (4 lb) free-range capon, jointed
150 g (5 oz) green streaky bacon, cut into cubes
20 small onions
125 g (4 oz) butter
½ glass cognac
1 litre (2 pints) red Burgundy
1 bouquet garni
2 cloves garlic
salt and pepper
1 tablespoon sugar
200 g (7 oz) small mushrooms
1 tablespoon flour
garlic croutons

Fry the chicken, bacon and onions in about 65 g (2½ oz) of the butter in a large pan. When they have started to brown, chuck in the cognac and flame. Pour on the red wine and add the bouquet garni, garlic, salt and pepper.

Bring to the boil, add the sugar, cover and simmer for approximately 3 hours or until the chicken is done. At the end of the cooking time heat the mushrooms in some butter.

Remove the chicken from the pan when it is done and keep warm. Discard the garlic and bouquet garni. Add the mushrooms to the sauce and simmer for 5 minutes.

Make a *beurre manié* with the remaining butter and the flour, and add it to the sauce little by little. Stir well until the sauce has thickened. Arrange the chicken pieces on a deep platter. Pour the sauce over and garnish with the garlic croutons. (From Burgundy.)

BARBECUED CHICKEN

from FAR FLUNG FLOYD

My chum Somchai organized a wonderful river trip in Mae Hong Son. We were tootling contentedly around a wide sweeping bend, filming as we went, when we encountered a spectacular sight. A boy of about twelve was wading across the river, bareback on an elephant.

It was a most impressive sight, rather spoiled by two boats of Japanese tourists who were so busy filming us that they practically drove into the elephant and caused it to stampede. Luckily the boy knew what to do, and got the terrified animal safely to the shore.

After that commotion, we pulled into the bank and before you could say Rudyard Kipling, Somchai had a fire going and was spit roasting chickens for our lunch.

SERVES 4

150 ml (¼ pint) cognac
2 tablespoons light soy sauce
2 tablespoons coconut milk
1 tablespoon fish sauce
4 cloves garlic, chopped
1 tablespoon chopped fresh coriander – root or leaf
a little chopped fresh root ginger
salt
freshly ground black pepper
1.4 kg (3 lb) free-range chicken, split in half
    through the breastbone and backbone – or ask
    your butcher to do it for you
sliced raw vegetables of your choice, to garnish

Mix together the cognac, soy sauce, coconut milk, fish
sauce, garlic, coriander, ginger and seasoning. Rub this
marinade all over the chicken and leave for 30 minutes.

Then drain and cook the chicken in a preheated oven,
180°C/350°F (gas mark 4), for 40 minutes, until tender.
To give it a lovely crispy brown finish, whack it on a
barbecue or under a preheated hot grill for around 10–15
minutes. Serve with raw vegetables. (From Thailand.)

Meat Dishes

VEAL ESCALOPE WITH DIJON MUSTARD
Escalope de Veau à la Moutarde

from FLOYD ON FRANCE

SERVES 4

butter
4 thin veal escalopes
salt and pepper
1 glass cognac
150 ml (5 fl oz) double cream
1 tablespoon mild Dijon mustard
chicken stock (optional)

Melt some butter in a pan and, as it begins to turn nutty brown, fry the escalopes for 2 minutes on each side. Season with salt and pepper, pour in the cognac and flame. This will create quite a bit of juice in the pan, so take the meat out at once, so that it does not boil in the liquid, and keep warm. Turn down the heat. Now stir the cream briskly into the juices and add the mustard. If at this stage the sauce is too thick, add 1 tablespoon chicken stock or even water to thin it down.

Stir in a knob of butter, season with salt and pepper and strain over the meat. Serve with boiled rice and a crunchy green salad. (From Burgundy.)

PORK IN WALNUT SAUCE
Cerdo en Nogada

from FLOYD ON SPAIN

SERVES 4

900 g (2 lb) boneless loin of pork, as lean as
    possible, rolled and tied
sea salt
50 g (2 oz) butter
freshly grated nutmeg
freshly ground black pepper
1 tablespoon cognac
600 ml (1 pint) milk
100 g (4 oz) walnuts, shelled

4 small cooking apples, cored
25 g (1 oz) cornflour

Sprinkle the pork joint generously with the sea salt and leave it for an hour or so.

Rub half the butter over the pork and grate some nutmeg and pepper over it. (You could use ready-ground nutmeg at a pinch, but it doesn't taste a tenth as good. Invest in a nutmeg grater.)

Heat a deep flameproof casserole and pop in the pork joint; brown it well on all sides. Spoon in the cognac and set a match to it to flame the meat.

Transfer the pork to a roasting tin, pour over the milk and roast in a preheated oven, 200°C/400°F (gas mark 6), for 30 minutes. Then add the walnuts and cook for about another hour, until the meat is tender. Score the apples round their middles with a sharp knife and bake in the oven for the last 30 minutes or so on a separate dish with a knob of the remaining butter on each.

Lift out the pork. Thicken the pan juices with the cornflour, mixed with a little cold water, then strain the sauce into a jug. Carve the meat and serve it with the apples and some mashed potatoes. Hand round the sauce separately.

STUFFED BEEF OLIVES

Alouettes sans Têtes

from FLOYD ON FRANCE

SERVES 6

300 g (10 oz) lean pork, minced
1 small handful parsley, chopped
3 cloves garlic, minced
salt and pepper
1 kg (2 lb) stewing beef, cut into slices, beaten as
 thin as possible
2 tablespoons oil
750 g (1½ lb) tomatoes, peeled, de-seeded and
 chopped
2 tablespoons cognac
2 tablespoons flour
1 glass red wine
thyme

Mix the pork, parsley, 1 clove of garlic, salt and pepper together and distribute it evenly between the pieces of beef. Roll up and tie together with string or hold with a toothpick.

In a large saucepan or deep frying pan fry the rest of 43

the garlic in the oil with half the tomatoes. Add the meat parcels and carefully brown. Flame with the cognac and sprinkle with flour. Add the wine, remaining tomatoes, thyme, salt and pepper, and stir. Cover and cook gently for 2 hours. (From Provence.)

SIRLOIN STEAK WITH TRUFFLE SAUCE
Entrecôte Sauce Périgourdine

from FLOYD ON FRANCE

200 g (7 oz) sirloin steak per person
lard for frying

For the sauce:

butter
2 heaped tablespoons flour
75 ml (3 fl oz) Madeira
cognac
1 small shallot, finely chopped
50 g (2 oz) preserved truffles, chopped, juices
    reserved
pinch of thyme
salt and pepper

First make the sauce. Melt the butter in a heavy-bottomed pan. Add the flour and fry until pale brown. Pour in the Madeira, 150 ml (5 fl oz) water and a dash of cognac. Add the shallot, truffles and thyme. Simmer gently and reduce to a thick sauce, and add salt and pepper. Whisk in a nut of butter to finish the sauce.

Fry the steaks in the lard over a very hot flame and pour the sauce over.

Please, please, serve the steaks rare, so that when you cut the meat the juices will run into the truffle sauce and enrich it wonderfully. (From Périgord.)

PROVENÇAL BEEF STEW
Daube à la Provençale

from FLOYD ON FRANCE

This excellent beef stew from Provence benefits from slow cooking, in an earthenware pot with a good tight-fitting lid.

SERVES 6

2 kg (4 lb) good stewing beef, cut in chunks
250 g (8 oz) smoked streaky bacon, finely diced

oil

2 cloves garlic, chopped

2 tablespoons cognac

3 tablespoons flour

1 glass good red wine

2 tablespoons wine vinegar

For the marinade:

4 glasses good red wine

2 tablespoons vinegar

2 tablespoons garlic, finely chopped

1 sprig of thyme

3 cloves

1 bay leaf

1 small handful parsley, chopped

sea salt and black pepper

1 large onion, chopped

Combine the meat with all the marinade ingredients and leave overnight.

Fry the bacon in some of the oil with the garlic. Drain the meat, reserving the marinade, add to the bacon and brown all over. Pour over the warmed cognac and flame. Sprinkle on the flour and stir well. Pour on the marinade, wine and vinegar. Stir well and cover. Simmer gently for

3 hours, adding water if necessary. The sauce should be rich and thick, and spicy; the meat very tender.

Often this dish is served with plain boiled noodles sprinkled with grated cheese and black pepper. (From Provence.)

Puddings and Drinks

APPLE CAKE

Pastis

from FLOYD ON FRANCE

500 g (1 lb) flour, sifted
1 egg
2 pinches salt
1 tablespoon nut oil
125 g (4 oz) butter, melted
200 g (7 oz) caster sugar
½ glass cognac
1 cooking apple, peeled, cored and thinly sliced

Put the flour into a bowl and make a well in the centre. Add the egg, salt, oil and enough water to make a soft dough. With your fingertips, carefully incorporate the flour, little by little. Thoroughly knead the dough on a floured surface. Beat it with a rolling pin and throw it down several times. When the pastry is quite smooth and stretches without cracking, it is ready. Roll it up, oil it lightly and refrigerate for at least 4 hours.

Pre-heat the oven to gas mark 5, 190°C (375°F).

Cover a large table with a floured cloth. Shape the dough into a long baguette and then pull it into a large rectangle, with the dough as thin as possible. Allow to dry for 10 minutes. Paint it with some of the melted butter and sprinkle all over some of the sugar and cognac.

Butter a cake tin. Cut the pastry into six rounds slightly bigger than the tin. Line the tin with three layers of pastry and then the apple slices, sprinkled with more sugar and cognac. Cover with the other three rounds. Paint the surface with melted butter and dust with a little sugar. Cut the pastry remains into strips and use them to decorate the cake. Sprinkle with sugar and cognac and paint with butter. Bake for 30 minutes in the oven. (From Périgord.)

NUT TART

Gâteau aux Noix

from FLOYD ON FRANCE

For the pastry:

250 g (8 oz) flour, sifted
100 g (3½ oz) butter, softened

50 g (2 oz) caster sugar
2 egg yolks
pinch of salt

For the filling:

125 g (4 oz) fresh walnuts, chopped, or dried
    walnuts, ground
300 ml (10 fl oz) double cream
½ teaspoon vanilla essence
100 g (3½ oz) caster sugar
1 egg white, beaten until stiff
pinch of salt

For the icing:

50 ml (2 fl oz) cognac
100 g (3½ oz) icing sugar
10 walnut halves

Mix the pastry ingredients into a firm ball. Refrigerate for
1 hour before rolling out to 1 cm (½ in) thick.

Pre-heat the oven to gas mark 4, 180°C (350°F).

Line a pie dish with the pastry and pop into the oven
until it hardens, without browning.

Meanwhile, combine all the filling ingredients and fill
the pie shell with the mixture. Return to the oven at gas

mark 5, 190°C (375°F), for 35 minutes. While the tart is cooking, mix the icing sugar with the cognac. When it is cooked, allow to cool, then ice it with this mixture and decorate with the walnut halves. (From Périgord.)

CHARENTE VANILLA CAKE
Le Milla

from FLOYD ON FRANCE

1 cup cornflour, sifted
1 cup plain flour, sifted
1½ cups milk
1½ cups caster sugar
25 g (1 oz) dried yeast
2 packets vanilla sugar
¼ glass cognac
pinch of salt
125 g (4 oz) butter, melted
2 eggs, beaten

Pre-heat the oven to gas mark 7, 220°C (425°F).

Mix everything together well, adding the butter and eggs last. Pack the mixture into a pie dish, drizzle a little melted butter over the top and sprinkle with a little flour. Bake in the oven for 35 minutes. (From Charente.)

PRUNE ICE CREAM WITH COGNAC
Helado de Ciruela con Coñac

from FLOYD ON SPAIN

This is a super pudding that is made commercially in Spain, but is best of all when home-made.

SERVES 6–8

1 litre (1¾ pints) vanilla ice cream
100 g (4 oz) stoned prunes, soaked overnight in
  125 ml (4 fl oz) cognac
125 ml (4 fl oz) cognac

Take the vanilla ice cream out of the freezer for about 10 or 15 minutes to soften it, otherwise you'll have a problem trying to mix the prunes with a frozen brick.

In the meantime, put the prunes into a small saucepan with their soaking liquid and a little water and simmer gently for 10 minutes. Drain, reserving the liquid, and chop them.

Put the softened ice cream into a large bowl, mix with

a wooden spoon for a moment to even out the consistency and fold in the chopped prunes. Pop back into its container and return to the freezer to harden.

Mix the reserved prune juice with the second lot of cognac and serve this potent sauce poured over the ice cream.

PS You could try this recipe with dried apricots instead of prunes – another dazzling combination.

SANGRÍA

There are many variations but the basic recipe is made with red wine, cognac, cinnamon, bits of fruit and some fizz (for example, fizzy orange, lemon or soda). If you want to make it stronger add more hard alcohol. Make sure it is served icy cold – allow plenty of time for it to chill in the refrigerator.

MAKES ABOUT I LITRE (I ¾ PINTS)

1 lemon, thinly sliced
1 orange, thinly sliced
1 apple, diced

1 pear, diced
banana liqueur
Cointreau
Cognac
*1 bottle of dry, full-bodied red wine (we used Viña
    Chiringuito)*
1 small bottle fizzy orange, chilled
1 small bottle fizzy lemon, chilled
1 teaspoon sugar
1 cinnamon stick
Ice cubes

Put the lemon and orange slices with the diced apple and
pear into as large a jug as you can find. Then add a generous
amount of the banana liqueur, Cointreau and cognac. Pour
in the bottle of wine and leave to chill thoroughly. When
the drink is really cold, pour in the fizzy orange and lemon
and add the sugar and cinnamon stick. Throw in a few ice
cubes, pour into some glasses and drink it.

THE CORPSE REVIVER

from FLOYD ON HANGOVERS

There's nothing like a good dose of 'hair of the dog' to aid a swift recovery when you're finding the morning after a touch painful! Fernet Branca is a nattily bottled medicinal drink from Milan, which has been around for one hundred and fifty years. Like the German hangover cure, Underberg, it contains over forty selected herbs, has a high alcohol content and is good for promoting the flow of the gastric juices and giving a sense of well being. In fact, the Savoy Hotel make an extremely interesting reviver based on Fernet Branca.

> *1 measure of cognac*
> *1 measure of Fernet Branca*
> *1 measure of white crème de menthe*

Put all the ingredients into a cocktail shaker with some ice. Shake and strain into a glass. Do not, under any circumstances, drive for the remainder of the morning.

THE PRAIRIE OYSTER

from FLOYD ON HANGOVERS

The following cure is probably the most famous morning-after reviver of all time.

1 measure of cognac
1 tablespoon vinegar
1 tablespoon Worcestershire sauce
1 teaspoon tomato ketchup
1 teaspoon Angostura Bitters
pinch of cayenne
the yolk of 1 free-range egg

Mix together all the ingredients, apart from the cayenne and egg yolk, in a whisky glass. Add a small pinch of cayenne and drop in the nice orangey yolk of the free-range egg. I stress this because it is important to use only the best-quality and freshest eggs from producers whose hens have been Salmonella-tested. Drink down in one without breaking the yolk.